love like the french

Dedication

I dedicate this book to Nazaire, Maxime, Anais, Cecile, Marie-Neige, Lane Jones, Roxanne G., Jennifer, Angela, Jerilyn, Becky, Kislany Elizabeth, Madame Moreau, Wendy, Stephanie T, Arlene Denise, Dr. Marge Taylor, Tante Valentine "Valia," Jean-Marie, and Martine Lorente.

THE FRENCH CONNECTIONS PUBLISHING

The French Connection Publishing

thefrenchperspective.com

ISBN: 978-0-578-80593-1 (print)
ISBN: 978-0-578-80594-8 (ebook)
Ordering Information:
Special discounts are available on quantity purchases by corporations, associations, and others. For details, contact Guy.blaise77@gmail.com

Contents

love

like the

french

A GUIDE TO BETTER ROMANCE AND RELATIONSHIPS

GUY BLAISE

Introduction

My name is Blaise. I was partially raised by my maternal grand-mother, Elizabeth, who is now 92 years old and lives in Bordeaux, in the western part of France. She became a widow in her early forties with young daughters and sons. Elizabeth took on the role of father and mother to her own children, and later she took on the added responsibility of helping raise her grandchildren, my siblings, and me. She often referred to death as the thief that stole her husband and the father of her children. In my teenage years, I became Elizabeth's confidant and protector. Sometimes I would ask her why she didn't remarry. Her answer was always, "Your grandfather was the love of my life, and it would be impossible to replace him." Her words have never left me all these years and still resonate in my ears. Perhaps, to some degree, I have always sought the type of relationship where we make each other feel irreplaceable.

In my youth, I was witness to my sisters' and aunts' dating experiences, and I listened closely to the advice my grandmother routinely gave them about relationships and love. America's *People* magazine was influential among my aunts' and older siblings' generation in France. They would pass it around to one another and admire the beauty, the fashion, and the relationships. There was always talk of boys and marriage. Elizabeth would remind the young women not to rush into a serious relationship too soon. When my older sister, Solange, married, her husband reached out to our grandmother when they began having problems in the relationship. Solange earned many of our grandmother's lectures for the negotiating tactics she used when solving problems in their marriage. My sister used sex to always get her way in the relationship; compromising was rarely an option. Not long ago, my aunt, Emilienne, went to visit her mother with news of her recent engagement. Without hesitation, Elizabeth asked Emilienne to go home and return the next day. Aunt Emilienne was disappointed at the response but did as her mother asked. The next day, Emilienne could not wait to hear her mother's explanation for why she sent her home. Elizabeth explained that she wanted to give Emilienne an extra day to think about her decision to marry. She told her that marriage is not easy and that it is important to choose a partner wisely.

When I began dating, my grandmother severely called me out and punished me for calling my girlfriend a *pute* (French for "whore") during an argument. Elizabeth made sure the word left a bad taste in my mouth. You can imagine my surprise the first time a lover asked me to use the word in bed. Intimacy among the French commonly involves profanity.

I have always kept in mind the advice my grandmother gave the women in the family. I dated multiple girls. I was convinced it wasn't a good idea to get into a relationship with the first available girl. I needed to see the world, make mistakes, and learn from them. Moving to America, being single, I find that my acts of chivalry, which are expected in France, are received with surprise in America. It is clear that there are differences in the dating norms between American and French women.

The interactions between my grandmother, my sisters, and my aunts provided a great deal of information for an observant young man with an insatiable curiosity. My upbringing exposed me to the French woman's perspective on every subject imaginable. I am eternally grateful to the strong women in my family, my grandmother in particular, for helping me become the man I am today.

After writing *Vive la Différence: A Frenchman's Perspective on American Women, Love, Respect, and Relationships*, I received letters from readers asking questions on subjects they had hoped to see in the book. I collected these questions and reflected on responses that resulted in the book you are reading today.

Just as those questions were candid and honest, I made an effort to offer responses written with equal candor and honesty. From one end of the world to the other, there is no shortage of relationship angst. It is a quality that unites us regardless of our gender, upbringing, or where we reside.

As with my prior book, these answers are not the work of a relationship expert. They are merely my heartfelt perspective as a man who grew up with the influence of strong women. It is my hope that everyone who reads this book will take something from it that they can apply to their own lives.

Letter 1

Do French men like sending unsolicited dick pics as much as American men?

Emma
Saint Paul, MN

Dear Emma,

You say in America that the apple never falls far from the tree. Sex and the penis are never far from each other. This is the same among men in both France and America. Large or small, circumcised or uncircumcised, thick or thin, straight or curved, penises all have one thing in common: They are valuable treasures for the men who own them. Most of us give our penis a nickname. Or better yet, a lover will give it a name for us, preferably a name that alludes to our ability to satisfy sexually.

Men send dick pics for a variety of reasons. Some men are looking for validation. Others do it to send a message. The message says, "This is what I have to offer you. This is what I bring to the bedroom for your pleasure." A dick pic is a man's misguided way of offering you the chance to imagine the many orgasms you could experience if you were to give him the opportunity. There are also those who send dick pics because they are proud of their dick's size and enjoy showing them off. I recall seeing a picture sent to a coworker of a box of Magnum condoms. The sender wanted her to know that his dick was larger than average, thereby requiring larger-than-average condoms. The man was under the impression that bigger meant he was better in bed. Having a penis does not guarantee you will give a woman an orgasm, but men want to make it clear that they have what it takes to keep you sexually satisfied. In addition, a compliment or a positive response of any kind from a woman is quite the ego booster.

When discussing dick pics with American and French women, I discovered that millennial women in both American and France receive more unsolicited dick pics than other age groups. Men who believe their dick size and appearance are an asset are more likely to put their dicks on display to lure or impress the recipient. Another reason for the unsolicited dick pic is immaturity. A confident, mature man will not find it necessary to share a picture of his genitals to attract a woman's attention but, rather, he will rely on his intellect, humor, and accomplishments. Sadly, immaturity can be found at any age.

I want to share with you how many French women handle the unsolicited dick pic. They keep a picture in their phones of a banana or a carrot stabbed with a knife. From what I hear, it is a very effective reply with a clear message. American women should respond in the same way.

"Le pénis c'est comme une balle de golf, il cherche toujours un trou." — *Dan Franco*

"The penis is like a golf ball; it always looks for a hole."

If we are fortunate, we become wiser with age. There was a time when I would oblige a woman's request for a dick pic, although never unsolicited. The French are much less inhibited than Americans when it comes to nudity. I never saw a problem with anything intimate shared between two consenting adults. I have also had past lovers request videos of our lovemaking. I did not refuse them either. The common reason for the request was to have something to remember me by or to masturbate with on the days we were not together.

Today, I am older and a little wiser, and I would not be so quick to oblige such intimate requests made by strangers. In fact, a stranger's reaction to being turned down may be very telling about who they are. Not having the ability to go back in time means I have to live with my mistakes and hope to make better decisions moving forward.

Letter 2

My greatest fantasy is to have a ménage à trois with my husband. I suspect he would be open to the idea if it were me and another woman, but I want us to be with another man. I haven't discussed it with him because part of me is worried he will lose his mind at the very thought. Given that the word is French, does that mean they are common in French culture? How would you suggest I approach my husband with the idea?

Priscilla
Brooklyn, NY

Dear Priscilla,

There are many women who crave to be the center of interest between two men. In general, French women are sexually liberated. They are very comfortable turning their sexual fantasies into reality. Two men, two cocks, and four hands imply double the pleasure. It would not surprise me if women fantasized about a ménage à trois with two men as often as men fantasize about having them with two women.

I'm afraid my opinion will not weigh heavily on what your husband wants. Your husband may have fantasies of his own that he is afraid to share with you. Keep in mind that even if your husband agrees, it is possible that the experience could leave the relationship vulnerable to jealousy and other problems, especially if the other man turns out to be a fantastic lover. Your husband will not be able to resist comparing himself to your guest. The thought of losing our partners to a better lover is a terrifying concept for men. Even if all goes well, he may begin to wonder if you are seeing the other man without him. It is also possible that your curiosity may grow and that you might decide you need to see the other man privately.

I suggest you test the waters by finding a way to bring up the topic in general, perhaps as a discussion related to a book you are reading. If the gentleman doesn't want to share, respect his wishes as you would expect him to do in return. I would also reassure your husband that this fantasy is not because he is not enough for you. Tell him that you had this fantasy long before meeting him. If he is undecided, consider watching porn with him first; maybe it will pique his interest. Another thing to consider is to offer him in exchange the opportunity to fulfill one of his fantasies. After all, fair is fair. If he does agree, rules need to be established in advance about how far you will go sexually so that your husband doesn't feel left out or surprised by anything that happens during the rendezvous.

"C'est celui dont tu as soigné l'impuissance qui te prend ta femme." — Malian Proverb

"It is the one who you have cured of sexual impotence who takes your wife from you."

Letter 3

My husband gives me the silent treatment when he is mad. Is that common behavior in French men as well, and how do you suggest I handle it?

Helen
Alexandria, OH

Dear Helen,

Silence can be a language of wisdom. Sometimes a man needs time to reflect on an argument before reacting. Think about your husband's character. How does he react to conflict in general? He may need time to process his feelings about what just happened. Imagine if every man in the world stepped away from an argument or confrontation with his partner before reacting; it would likely result in a drastic decline in domestic abuse. Of course, it is also possible that your husband is using the silent treatment as a form of punishment, a way of showing his discontent with your words or actions. If punishment is the reason, then he is displaying a level of immaturity that is unacceptable and will lead to further problems in the relationship.

Many French women use the silent treatment to punish their partners when they are angry. It is also a way for them to say, without actually saying it, "You don't deserve my attention right now." As for French men, we do not have an aversion to communication or to expressing our feelings. In fact, we love to talk things out with our partners. We need to talk. We need to know how our partners are feeling. For us, the silent treatment is excruciating, hence the reason so many French women love to use it.

After reading your question, I called my Aunt Philomene in Montpellier in the south of France and asked her about your situation. Her first husband was notorious for giving her the silent treatment. Her answer was quite sincere. "I would just let him go in his own direction and make his own choices without being his obstacle. When he was ready to communicate with me, he would let me know. I would rather give him the time he needs than argue with someone angry and unreasonable."

I would suggest you play indifference to his silence and see if it changes his behavior. If indifference doesn't change his behavior, then he truly needs time to gather his thoughts and process his feelings before responding.

"La patience est amère, mais son fruit est doux."
— French Proverb

"Patience is bitter, but its fruit is sweet."

Letter 4

My husband's family drives me crazy. They are too involved in our personal life. How do I stop them from being so invasive without offending them?

Claudine
Metairie, LA

Dear Claudine,

It is often said that when you marry someone, you marry their family. We say in French, "*Tu aimes le chien, aime aussi ses puces*" ("If you like the dog, you must also like his fleas"). This can be especially difficult with spouses who are extremely close to their siblings or parents. This type of overstepping can lead to unwanted competition between the wife and the mother-in-law, forcing the husband to feel stuck in the middle.

It is clear that there were no boundaries set at the very beginning of your relationship with your husband's family. Ideally, when you marry into a new family, you learn about each other and set unspoken boundaries along the way. There can be a fine line between being a close-knit family and being involved in overly personal matters. Unfortunately, it will be more difficult to stop the meddling than it would have been to avoid it in the first place. Changing your husband's family's behavior will require intentional communication from him. Trying to resolve this yourself will only lead to family conflict. The delicate conversations that need to happen to stop your husband's family from continuing to cross boundaries must come directly from your husband, as it is his family. If his family is being reasonable, they will understand your position and back away without taking offense. When a husband and wife unite, they become a separate entity or an extension of their respective original families. Therefore, it is completely up to you and your husband to decide how much or how little involvement his family has in your life. Sometimes it is necessary to put your foot down with family members who are not respecting your boundaries. Have a discussion with your husband about what is and isn't acceptable so that you're both on the same page before addressing his family.

In-laws can be a valuable support system but they can also be a nightmare. Who you end up with is a matter of luck. I am not suggesting to keep them at a distance, because a couple can still benefit from their advice, especially couples who are newlyweds or new parents. In France, just like in America, grandparents can be a great resource of support, often giving the parents a much-needed break by taking the grandchildren and allowing the parents to spend quality time together as a couple without their children.

I have great respect for in-laws who are not invasive, those who have accepted playing a secondary role in the life of their son/daughter and who do not see their son's wife, or daughter's husband, as a threat.

"On mesure l'union d'une famille par sa capacité à traverser ensemble les moments difficiles." — *Clement Auray*

"We measure the union of a family by its ability to go through difficult times together."

Letter 5

My husband doesn't show any appreciation for all that I do for him and the family. Any suggestions? A little appreciation would be nice!

Ashley
Edmond, OK

Dear Ashley,

Showing appreciation to your partner is a way to show respect. I often hear Americans say that "women are the nurturers." This statement gives men an easy out. It takes them off the hook from contributing to household chores and puts them in a position of dependency. Men may not feel a need to contribute to household duties when they perceive women to be the nurturers and, therefore, better at accomplishing these tasks.

The truth is a man would find a way to feed himself, wash his own clothes, and clean his own space if he didn't have someone to do it for him. Of course, there are men who are perfectly content to wallow in their own filth, but for the most part, we want pleasant living conditions like everyone else.

Being a good wife doesn't mean doing everything for your husband. If your husband is not showing you any appreciation, treat that problem the way you would treat any other issue in the relationship, with communication. Have a discussion about your feelings and what you need from your partner. A woman should never assume that saying something in general terms will be enough for a man. You might already tell your husband, "I don't feel appreciated," but are you providing specific examples of how he can show you his appreciation? It may sound silly or unnecessary to you but men often prefer a level of preciseness that leaves nothing to interpretation. Interpretation, as you know, can vary greatly from one person to the next.

Allow your partner the time and grace to correct the error of his ways, and don't forget to lead by example. A loving relationship requires consideration from both partners.

"Un chien reconnaissant vaut mieux qu'un homme ingrat."
— French Proverb

"A grateful dog is better than an ungrateful man."

Letter 6

My husband is gone all the time. Am I being unreasonable to want him home more often?

Sandy
Austin, TX

Dear Sandy,

C'est la vie! I will not rush to judgment since you haven't provided any reasons for your husband's absence. There are men who work hard to provide for their families. Sometimes this requires having more than one job. Presuming he is at work, the challenge is how to find the balance between professional obligations and family. Even in a family-friendly country like France with easily accessible day care, it is still difficult to balance work and family life. Now if your husband is gone all the time for the wrong reasons, this is a different matter altogether. Is he avoiding you? Is he having an affair? Is he selfishly spending too much time doing things that only interest him? If he is working long hours, then his absence should be supported by the extra money he is bringing home.

My advice to you is to reflect on your relationship. Disregarding the time you are apart, how do the two of you interact when you are together? Therein lies the answer to your question. Are you both genuinely connecting when you are under the same roof? If your emotional bond is still strong and your husband has valid reasons to be away often, then I would not worry. I would, however, make time to discuss with your partner how you feel about the distance. Perhaps, there are some changes that can be made once your spouse is aware of your unhappiness. It may be time to examine the quality of the time you spend together and reevaluate the priorities within your relationship. Love shouldn't die because a husband is working hard to take care of his family.

"L'absence ne tue l'amour que s'il est malade au départ."
— Roger de Bussy-Rabutin

"Absence only kills love if it is sick at the start."

Letter 7

I miss sex with my ex-husband. What do you think I should do?

Amy
Eagle Creek, OR

Dear Amy,

An ex is an ex for a reason. Depending on the circumstances of the separation, some people choose to remain friends, while others prefer to sever ties completely, particularly when they are involved in new relationships. Personally, I am not surprised by the feeling of missing sex with your ex-husband, especially if he knew how to please you in bed. I will say that few men will turn down an invite for sex, especially if it is initiated by an ex-lover. Consider the risks involved in that behavior. Not knowing if you are involved with someone, it is hard to give you my opinion. Are you currently in a new relationship? If so, will returning to your ex help you become a better lover to your new partner? Would a physical reunion bring up old feelings for each other? While there is comfort in familiarity, there are other factors to consider when we go backward instead of moving ahead. My advice is to focus on your future and on building a new relationship that involves teaching your new partner exactly what curls your toes in the bedroom. French women are very outspoken about their sexual needs. They are not shy about correcting and instructing their lovers. American women should be just as outspoken as their French sisters. Returning to a broken relationship for sex will keep you in the past, and the odds of it lasting are slim to none.

"L'herbe est toujours plus verte où elle est arrosée.»
— French Proverb

"The grass is greener where it is watered."

Letter 8

My significant other, the father of my children, attended an event in Florida last week. He said that less than half of the attendees wore masks to prevent spreading COVID-19. When he returned, I refused to let him get near us and forced him to self-quarantine in the basement. We have two young children who I have to consider as well. To make matters worse, last night he begged me to have sex and told me he didn't mind if we both wore masks while we did it. He also assured me that I couldn't catch the virus through semen. As a man yourself, do you see this as typical male behavior or am I living with an asshole?

Ruthie
Columbia, SC

Dear Ruthie,

Your letter gave me goosebumps. I'm curious to know your partner's age because he seems egocentric and immature. Abstaining from sex during a quarantine period will not cause his penis to rust and fall off! Sex is not food; he will not die if he goes without. Evidently, he is not considering the danger of infecting the mother of his children or the risk of contaminating the children themselves. There may be no proof that he is infected, but given his exposure, there is reason to be cautious. Even if he is physically doing well after his trip to Florida, he can still be in the incubation phase of the disease.

I understand the frustration of not having sex, especially if your partner is someone who is not used to going without, but this an exceptional time. There are many contradicting reports on men's semen and COVID-19 transmissions. No one knows with certainty. Even if the virus is not sexually transmitted, how would sex work with a mask? Speaking as a French man, I cannot imagine making love to my partner without kissing her and doing things to make us both breathe heavily while in close proximity to one another.

It looks to me as if you will have to be the voice of reason because your husband is not thinking with his head on straight.. As a man, I can tell you that men respect women who respect themselves. Protect yourself and your children. Your husband, the asshole, is free to masturbate until he gets tested.

"Les femmes qui souffrent le plus des maris gâtés ce sont celles qui les gâtent." — French Proverb

"The women who suffer the most from spoiled husbands are the ones who spoil them."

Letter 9

I am a Black woman married to a White man. I find that we encounter the most racism from strangers in the street, white women in particular. Have you ever been in an interracial relationship and, if so, is there as much racism in France as there is in America?

Chantal
Arlington Heights, IL

Dear Chantal,

Crossing racial barriers is seen as a transgression for some people. There are looks on the streets that never lie. The lips are silent but the eyes glare accusingly, "You couldn't find someone of your own race?" Sadly, racism is an equal-opportunity display of ignorance that does not confine itself to borders of any kind.

Yes, I have crossed racial barriers many times in my relationships.

France is proud of its reputation for being the pioneer of human rights. We have an open-door policy that accepts anyone who is experiencing persecution of any form, including racism. For this reason, racism in France tends to happen in more discrete ways than what we see in America. For example, you might experience racism in the form of your job application getting passed over because your surname is not French. Another example might be the presumption that a person of color in a business can't be in a supervisory position. I cannot guarantee that you and your husband would not experience racism in France but I will say that publicly, the French are more accepting of interracial love. My experience with racism and interracial relationships in America has been that the more love and contentment your relationship demonstrates, the more appalled the racists become. To that I say, let them get angry. Your relationship shows open-mindedness and tolerance. Bravo!

I met Ellen on a dating site. She was very beautiful. After reading her profile, I decided to leave her a "Bonjour, Ellen" note. I checked my messages daily, hoping to see a response. A week later, she wrote back to me in French with an apology for taking so long to reply. I was seduced by her courtesy. My online profile did not include a picture. I was not comfortable displaying my identity online. I could see her pictures. She was very beautiful.

She shared with me that she loved France, loved the French language, and was excited to practice her French.

We exchanged at least 10 messages each day. Weeks passed, and Ellen never asked me for a picture. We were getting closer to each other and considering our first rendezvous.

Ellen and her 12-year-old daughter were taking French lessons together. Having daughters similar in age gave us one more thing in common. Our friendship intensified and our messages became intimate. Ellen soon began calling me her *cheri* ("darling").

Weeks of conversation and sharing details of our lives together led to meeting in person. We picked a weekend to meet at the library. It was the morning of our first meeting when she finally asked for my picture. I sent her a picture of me taken in Versailles.

Three hours later, I received an email from her apologizing for not being able to meet with me. She said she could not date a man of color. Ellen assumed that because I was French, I was White. She told me that her family would disown her if she dated me. She apologized repeatedly for her racism. And just like that, I was no longer her *cheri*. I thanked her for her honesty, and we never spoke again.

"Le couples mixtes sont les meilleurs atouts de notre humanité." — Monsieur-le-milliardaire

"Mixed couples are the best assets to our humanity."

Letter 10

I am engaged to my best friend and was so excited to become his wife. Recently, I was shocked to find gay porn on his laptop. Is it possible that a straight man would enjoy watching gay porn?

Evelyn
Bell Gardens, CA

Dear Evelyn,

Your discovery is a major one. I don't know of any straight man who would go to gay porn sites to find inspiration on how to sexually gratify a woman. The only time straight men are comfortable with or turned on by gay porn is when it involves only women.

Presuming you two are sexually active and you are not entering a marriage of convenience, there are two possibilities. Your fiancé is either gay or bisexual. "Better to know than to doubt," we say in French.

I am reminded of something a friend shared with me about her gay brother. He lived in a community that was predominantly Arab-American. The consequences of being a gay man in their culture can be severe. Rather than coming out, many will marry women and have children as their tradition dictates. My friend's brother had no shortage of lovers who would meet him discreetly, without strings or fear of emotional entanglements. On more than one occasion, he would run into a lover with his wife and children while going for a walk in the neighborhood. Unfortunately, hiding like this is a reality for some and even those in their circles are oblivious to the truth.

You and your fiancé have a lot to discuss. Be prepared for a conversation that may change the dynamic of your relationship. Above all, you deserve to know the truth.

"Pour savoir, il faut demander." — *French Proverb*

"To know, you have to ask."

I once dated a woman who I thought I knew quite well. We lived together for several years. One night, I woke up out of a sound sleep and noticed she wasn't next to me. I got out of bed and went to find her. In the room farthest from our bedroom, I could see a faint light underneath the closed door. I stopped myself from calling her name. Instead, I opened the door as slowly and quietly as I could. To my surprise, I discovered my girlfriend on a video call having a very sexual conversation with another woman. When I spoke, she slammed her laptop shut but it was too late. There was no mistaking what was going on. In the days that followed, we had a series of intense conversations about her secret and our relationship. It made me realize that a lot of people in relationships suppress their sexual orientation. Our relationship eventually ended because her desire to be with women.

Letter 11

My husband wants to have sex multiple times a day. I love him, and I love sex, but sometimes I am just too tired. Am I wrong for turning him down?

Marylin
Dover, DE

Dear Marylin,

I must confess, my first thought was a bit insensitive. Your husband finds you attractive and enjoys making love to you. That seems like a good problem to have. In France, we call it being married to a rabbit. But after more careful consideration, I would say that it can be problematic when partners have very different libidos. It's unfortunate when women feel as though they have to make up excuses, such as the classic headache. I can't speak for your husband but I personally prefer to hear the truth.

A marriage license is not an unlimited sex pass. Either gender has the right to turn down their spouse when they are not in the mood. I recently read a study released by the University of Ohio in 2011 that found that a man thinks of sex 18.6 times a day, while a woman thinks of sex 9.9 times a day. I am not trying to defend your husband but am merely pointing out a difference in the genders. The irony of it all is that women with high libidos often have partners with low libidos. We rarely seem to pair up just right. That said, your husband should understand if you turn him down occasionally because you are tired or had a rough day. The truth about men is that we need to feel wanted by our partners. We need to know that we can turn you on. This acknowledgment is a boost to our egos. Another truth is that we sometimes simply have an intense urge to empty our balls and we crave that satisfying release. If all else is going well in the relationship, with the exception of you having to say no to sex occasionally, your husband should be respectful of your wishes, but please don't give him any grief if you find him masturbating on the days you turn him down. Masturbation is cheap and doesn't require preliminaries.

I am for peace within households. But household peace should not come at the expense of women. When lovemaking lasts too long, it is no longer love, it is a sacrifice. Better a well done and short shot than a bad one that lasts two hours.

"Le sexe c'est l'état d'urgence dans le pantalon d'un homme."
— *French Proverb*

"Sex is a state of emergency in a man's pants."

Letter 12

I am worried that my husband drinks too much. He gets drunk every evening after work and becomes verbally abusive to our children and me. I am desperate and don't know what to do.

Barbara
Algoma, WI

Dear Barbara,

I am touched by your letter. The first victims of alcoholism are the closest family. You are between two fires. On the one hand, you want to protect yourself and the children, while on the other hand you certainly want to help your husband.

Alcoholism is a difficult journey. My grandfather died of cirrhosis of the liver due to alcoholism. In France, it is estimated that there are 800,000 alcohol-related hospitalizations every year. It is very common in France to offer wine to a boy as a rite of passage, a symbolic demonstration of his entering manhood. This is a custom I do not endorse. Alcohol is so deeply ingrained in French culture that turning down a drink will result in others questioning your health. "Why don't you want to drink?" "Are you sick?"

Most people do not become alcoholics overnight. Your husband was likely drinking prior to marrying you and has since increased the frequency of his drinking. If you are worried that your husband is drinking too much, then he probably is.

Having an alcoholic spouse seems to me to be an unbearable way of living. As his wife, you will have to have a very uncomfortable conversation with your husband and hopefully convince him to seek help. Does alcoholism run in his family? This may be another point of discussion. Alcoholism does not discriminate and leaves a path of destruction in its wake. Everyone in your husband's life will be affected so don't be afraid to bring that up. My advice is that you act sooner rather than later and make every effort to intervene before his problem becomes more severe. You aren't being fair to him or to yourself to sit back and worry in silence. Alcohol doesn't make people drunkards; it is the people who overdrink who get drunk.

I hope that the fear of being alone and fear of the unknown won't prevent you from leaving him if he doesn't seek help. Sometimes it is good to be selfish. Sometimes it is better to be alone than badly accompanied. If your husband was himself a child of an alcoholic parent, often children watch and repeat later in their lives.

"Si tu épouses un soulard, tu épouses les disputes et les bagarres." — French Proverb

"If you marry a drunk, you marry arguments and fights."

Letter 13

I have recently had a bad breakup with my boyfriend of 10 years. I'm consumed by thoughts of what he might be doing now that he moved out. Any advice for a broken heart?

Isabella
Aurora, OR

Dear Isabella,

Healing takes time. Sometimes words are not enough to console a broken heart. As badly as you want to know what your ex is doing, ask yourself, how will this information help you heal? It seems more like self-inflicted torture to keep up with his activities.

While I don't know the reason for your breakup, I believe it is psychological suicide to follow an ex on social media to keep tabs on him. This behavior will make it almost impossible to turn the page and begin a new chapter.

I realize it is easier said than done but you have to move on with your life. You deserve to be happy, and time truly does heal wounds. Try to focus on yourself and make new plans that do not include the ex. I have heard women say, "Nothing helps you forget an old love like a new love." Perhaps, this is a theory worth exploring, or perhaps you should simply focus on you for now. Relationships take compromise. Think of things you didn't do while you were in your relationship because your partner wouldn't enjoy them. Consider taking a class on something that interests you. The best is yet to come.

"Une rupture est comme un miroir brisé. Il vaut mieux le laisser brisé que de se blesser en tentant de le réparer."
— French Proverb

"A breakup is like a broken mirror. It is better to leave it broken than to injure yourself trying to repair it."

Letter 14

How do you feel about younger men dating older women?

Denise
Durham, NC

Dear Denise,

Personally, I have always been quite fond of mature women, even when I was much younger. Younger men who have romances with older women know a great secret. I have been in their shoes many times, and I do not mind sharing that secret with you.

I will give you a little background first. I am an intellectual dreamer with never-ending curiosity. This makes maturity and life experiences attractive to me. Imagine my surprise when a much-older woman showed interest in me as a young man in my twenties. She was a fount of wisdom. I looked at her and saw a library filled with books of all genres. Every line in her face held a story. She was a great source of knowledge about life and the world. She was a radiant woman full of energy, reserved, with the ability to keep her feelings under control. She had lived long enough to know exactly how she wanted to portray herself to the world, with class and style. I looked forward to every moment she allowed me to spend in her presence. When she looked at me, I knew she was about to tell me what she wanted, directly and without nonsense. She possessed an open-mindedness in the bedroom that made exploration anticipated and explosive. The time spent outside of the bedroom was nearly equally explosive. I relished listening to her views on life and the stories that sculpted those views, both good and bad. I used her experiences as I would a flashlight for my own life. She offered me a sense of safety and adventure I never felt when dating a woman younger than myself. This woman was very independent and did not need me; she wanted me. There is a vast difference between the two.

What did I offer her? Certainly, at that age, I did not have the wisdom or experience to match her own. But what I did have was a thirst for knowledge that absorbed her stories like a sponge. I had questions and genuine interest in her life lessons. I gave her comfort when she wanted to rest in my arms. I gave her the body, strength, and stamina that a man her age could not. Yes, I became that stereotypical boy toy, and yet there was nothing typical about it. She did not look at me as a long-term partner. I was a source of enjoyment in the present, even if she did love me to some degree. I am not suggesting that a relationship with a great difference in age cannot be long term. It just wasn't what happened to me. Nevertheless, it was a beautiful, satisfying relationship filled with love, respect, and unforgettable memories.

I would advise men and women of any age not to limit themselves when seeking relationships. Even when the standards of society do not share your views, you can become a contributor to change. Maturity is attractive on any continent. I see no difference between the confident, mature women I meet in the afternoons on the Champs Élysées in Paris and those I meet on 9th Street in Durham, North Carolina.

"Vive la vie et vive l'amour!" Long live life and long live love!

"L'amour n'a pas d'âge, c'est pourquoi les cheveux blancs ne poussent pas dans le Cœur." — French Proverb

"Love has no age, which is why gray hair doesn't grow on the heart."

Letter 15

I realize now that I don't know my husband at all. I feel like I am quarantined with a stranger. Is this feeling unusual or as global as the pandemic?

Ruth
Eliot, ME

Dear Ruth,

Do not put your husband up for sale on eBay just yet. Let's be a little bit optimistic. There are only two ways this forced confinement will go for couples: Their love for each other will be reinforced or it will break them. During these hard times, masks will fall and quarantine becomes a sort of test for couples on many levels. For those who may have rushed into a relationship or didn't take the time to truly get to know their partners, it is a real time of discovery.

Think back to when you first met. What about your husband made you fall in love? Why did you marry him? Once you get over the realization that you don't know each other very well, you can focus on something more positive. Get to know each other on a deeper level.

Time spent in quarantine is not the same for everyone. If your source of income was not affected, you are fortunate. Studies suggest that finances are the leading cause of stress in relationships. Many people have voiced how positive the extra time spent with family has been for them.

It is in my nature to see the glass half full, to look for the positive in every situation. Now that you have more time together, get to know that stranger you married. Share your concerns with him. You might discover that he feels the same about you. Your honesty can result in a more meaningful and intentional conversation.

Here is a game you could play. Write down questions that would help you learn about each other on strips of paper, fold them and toss them in a hat, and then take turns selecting questions. Set up a table to resemble a nice restaurant, order takeout, and have a quarantine date night. Start a couples' book club with other friends. You could read books that strengthen relationships and meet virtually to discuss. A friend of mine taught his wife to play poker during quarantine, and she is currently teaching him to play chess. Confinement is what you make of it. It is not fatal, especially if you choose to respect your differences. There is no such thing as a perfect husband or a perfect wife.

"Avec le temps les maris changent, certains mûrissent, d'autres pourrissent." — Blaise

"Over time husbands change. Some ripen, others rot."

I refuse to let the divorce rate in France or in America discourage me in any way from finding my forever partner. I love the idea of being married and being someone's husband and having a wife. For me, marriage offers emotional stability. I am not so naïve as to think that every day will be a honeymoon; marriage isn't a decision to enter into lightly. But when you are with the right person, there is nothing like it. Two people in love, working to stay together and striving to make each other happy, is magic.

Letter 16

It seems to me that having high standards makes it harder to find a relationship. Do you think we should lower our standards as we get older if we truly want to find a partner in life?

Wendy
Montpelier, VT

Dear Wendy,

You are the only one who knows if you are truly being discerning or just overly picky. If your standards are reasonable and realistic, I cannot imagine that you would be content to lower them, regardless of age. Some standards should never be lowered. On the other hand, if one of your criteria is that your partner must be over six feet tall, then that is one I would consider re-evaluating.

If you have ever used a dating site, you know that many of them offer compatibility questions. Some sites will tell you that being too rigid with your preferences in a partner will lower your number of possible matches.

We all know relationships take effort and compromise. Why put in the work for someone who is not up to your standards? My grandmother, Elizabeth, used to tell her daughters, my aunts, to see any relationship like a lime coated with honey. At the beginning it is sweet, then things turn sour. It requires both people to add another coat of honey to keep the relationship sweet. Personally, I would hate to go through life coating limes with a woman who feels she settled for me.

Since I do not know your standards, I suggest you write them down. Yes, make a list! You should write them down for the same reason nutritionists ask their clients to keep a food journal. It is different to know something inside your own head than it is to see it on paper. Better yet, write each standard on a sticky note. Then sort them into two categories; make one column for standards that are nonnegotiable and one column for standards to reevaluate. Out of curiosity, I asked a friend to share some of her standards and how she would categorize them. She said she wouldn't mind being flexible on looks, religion, or financial stability. However, she will not compromise on intelligence, sense of humor, or smoking. Another friend confided that she cannot be in a relationship with a man who is not well-endowed. This may not be a deal-breaker for many women but for her it is nonnegotiable.

Wendy, spend some time evaluating your needs and do not lower your standards in an attempt to increase your number of matches. Be honest with yourself; you will be glad for this in the long run. In the meantime, continue to challenge and love yourself for you. A partner should be a person who enhances our already-fulfilling lives, not someone we rely on for our happiness.

Being French and Black in America has been an interesting experience, especially when dating. I met Stephanie a few years ago through mutual friends. She found herself single after two failed marriages. Stephanie came from a conservative WASP household with a very racist father. Prior to meeting me, she never considered dating outside of her race. So why did Stephanie make an exception for me? She did it because I am French. This was not a one-time experience for me. In America, my Frenchness supersedes my Blackness.

We arranged to meet in the park for our first date. She loves France and spoke a little of the language. She couldn't wait to walk with me and practice her French. It was a beautiful, sunny day and we walked five miles enjoying each other's company. Whenever asked, I corrected her rusty French. At the end of our walk, we headed toward our parked cars. I pulled out a bottle of red Bordeaux from my car and presented it to her as I thanked her for a wonderful time. She was surprised by the gesture and said she had never received a gift on a first date. I assured her that my customs and I remain French, despite living in America.

For our second rendezvous, Stephanie invited me over to her house for dinner. She made a wonderful meal. After dinner, we moved to the porch, where the conversation led to a relaxing foot massage in appreciation for her work in the kitchen. The foot massage then led us to her bedroom.

As we became closer, she worried about introducing me to her father. One evening, back on the porch, sipping a Cabernet, she admitted to me that she was nervous about how her family would react to the news that she was dating a Black man. She told me that she had reached out to her siblings for advice. Her older sister was the only one to offer kind words. She told Stephanie, "If you truly believe in God, you believe that we are all His children and you will not discriminate."

As Stephanie became more comfortable with me, she made it abundantly clear that she would never fully let go of her racist and homophobic upbringing. Our romance ultimately ended because I was not willing to be the one exception to anyone's racism.

"L'amour rend aveugle mais le mariage redonne la vue."
— French Proverb

"Love blinds, but marriage gives the sight back."

Letter 17

My boyfriend is becoming increasingly critical. I'm beginning to feel as if he doesn't like me anymore, even though he claims to love me. Should I leave this relationship?

Susan
Adams, TN

Dear Susan,

If you are questioning whether or not you should stay in a relationship, you probably already know the answer. *Saying* and *doing* are two very different things.

Both partners in a relationship must speak the same language, in words and actions. Being overly critical is not a dealbreaker. Call your boyfriend out on his behavior. How does he react when you point out one of his mistakes? Most people are not bothered by someone pointing out their mistakes when it is done without malice.

Let's presume you decide your boyfriend is worth the effort of working on the relationship. You deserve to feel liked and loved by your boyfriend, and he deserves to know how he is making you feel. Give him an opportunity to make corrections. If he doesn't do anything differently, you have your answer.

"Il n'y a pas d'amour sans preuves d'amour."
— *French Proverb*

"There is no love without proof of love."

When I got married, my mother-in-law became the general manager of my marriage. All the way from her Frankfurt home, she held the remote that controlled her daughter from across the ocean. From day one of our marriage, I was the East Coast and my mother-in-law was the West Coast.

By the fifth year of marriage, my wife had become psychologically and verbally abusive. The last four years of my marriage were hell. My mother-in-law visited often and for extended periods of time. Her visits brought on stress and bouts of anxiety. While visiting, she would choose decorations for our home. She would tell us how things should be done and where things should go. I believe my mother-in-law's dislike for me influenced her daughter. The manipulation gradually increased. Mother and daughter teamed up in criticism. When they became tired of criticizing me, they would switch the conversation to German so that I could not understand. I was always either being criticized or ignored, and we certainly weren't having sex when the general manager was in town. My wife constantly belittled me and criticized me for everything. Despite working long hours, I would do my best to help around the house. I changed diapers at three in the morning. I rushed into bedrooms to scare off monsters whenever my name was called. I know what it feels like to never get anything right.

That experience taught me the value of a compliment. When you love someone, you never stop reminding them of how glad you are to have them in your life. The smallest act of appreciation refills the heart and strengthens the bond. As a person who always looks for the bright side of every situation, that is the one great lesson I learned from my experience.

Letter 18

My boyfriend expects me to give him a blow job every night. Is this a typical male expectation?

Jean
Aberdeen, ID

Dear Jean,

A blow job is not a human right, and it should never feel like an obligation. The best blow jobs in the world are the ones given by a partner who is truly enjoying the experience, not treating it like a chore. I expect to have a delicious meal when I go to a restaurant. This does not mean I always get it. Your boyfriend can expect anything he wants; how he reacts on the nights when his expectations are not met is what is most important. If he becomes upset or lays a guilt trip on you when you're not in the mood, then that is a cause for concern. Does he expect to go down on you as well or is this a one-sided expectation? Behaving with a sense of entitlement is not conducive to a healthy relationship. Refusing to suck your boyfriend's dick on command does not make you a bad girlfriend. I am amazed how often men behave like jerks to their women by day and then expect to be sexually gratified at night. What is the incentive for a woman to pleasure a man when he is not acting worthy of her touch? I am not suggesting your boyfriend is a jerk but I can't help wondering if there are other areas in the relationship where he behaves selfishly. Lovemaking is sharing and is most intense when it is organic and spontaneous.

"Une relation, c'est une réciprocité entre deux personnes. L'une ne doit pas tout donner et l'autre tout prendre."
— French Proverb

"A relationship is a reciprocity between two people. One must not give everything while the other takes everything."

Letter 19

My boyfriend comes from a wealthy family and is looking forward to a large inheritance. He treats me with disrespect and doesn't mind humiliating me in front of other people. Should I stay in this relationship knowing that he will be a good provider in the future?

Ana
Chapel Hill, NC

Dear Ana,

Thank you for your letter. I am sorry that you are not being treated right by your lover. As an observer of American society, I have seen women in similar circumstances more times than I care to admit. It seems that men like your boyfriend have no trouble attracting women. What does that say about the standards of women in general? If financial stability is number one on your list of requisites, then where do you place respect?

Someone I know personally endured many years with an abusive man of financial means. At the beginning of their relationship, she was a challenge for him, an acquisition. He made every effort to impress her with his charm, money, and status. Once the chase was over, his attention went elsewhere. I would guess about 15 percent of his late-night business meetings were actually about business. When he wasn't treating her like garbage, he was ignoring her. One day, she admitted to looking forward to their times together, even if they inevitably ended in arguments, because at least he was acknowledging her existence. What a sad way to live. Her relationship finally ended with a phone call from a disgruntled mistress, one of many.

I would be a liar if I said money is not important but money isn't everything. The fact that your partner is disrespectful to you and humiliates you in public speaks of his love, or lack thereof, toward you. My advice to you, Ana, is to revise your list of requisites and seek someone who treats you with love. There is no amount of money worth the sacrifice of your self-respect and happiness.

"L'argent fait beaucoup, mais l'amour fait tout."
— *French Proverb*

"Money does a lot, but love does everything."

Letter 20

My husband is unable to orgasm during penetration. He has to pull out after intercourse and then he masturbates until he comes. He tells me he has had this problem with all his previous relationships. Sometimes it makes me feel insecure and I wonder if he is just not sexually attracted to me. Is this normal?

Teresa
Durham, NC

Dear Teresa,

In the minds of many men, there is a direct correlation between *being a man* and our capacity to perform in bed. Our penises are important. French and Italian men are forever at odds over who is the better lover. There are a lot of factors that may be affecting your husband. Like an escargot hiding in its shell, men avoid the subject of sexual performance and have too much ego to seek the help of professionals. No matter what the cause, your reaction and reassurance will be extremely important to him. I cannot speak to the frequency of your experience, but I cannot imagine a reason why your husband would lie about having the same experience with his former lovers. I do urge that you encourage him to see his doctor to rule out any medical reasons for his problem.

Let's say your husband receives a clean bill of health and there is no medical reason for his inability to ejaculate inside you. What's next? I would bet that if you asked your husband what is most important to him, he would say it is pleasing you. My "glass half-full" perspective says your husband does not have to worry about climaxing too soon, something that many men have to make an effort to prevent from happening. Your husband can take you like the Energizer Bunny to your heart's content. Don't let him leave your bed to finish on his own. Try making his ejaculation a team effort, not a dirty little secret he has to accomplish alone. Have an honest discussion with him and reassure him that he is all the man you need.

"C'est n'est pas l'amour, qui dérange la vie, mais l'incertitude d'amour." —Francois Truffaut

"It's not love that disturbs life, but the uncertainty of love."

Letter 21

I recently admitted to my new boyfriend that I am bisexual. Now he is upset that I may leave him for a woman. How can I convince a straight man that I can be bisexual and still be faithful to him?

T
San Jose, CA

Dear T,

Being bisexual does not mean you are incapable of monogamy. Your ability to be faithful is not determined by which gender you're attracted to. With that said, I completely understand your boyfriend's insecurity. He is thinking he now has twice the competition and you have twice the temptation. In reality, if you have never given him a reason to doubt your loyalty to the relationship, then your boyfriend should give you the benefit of the doubt. Perhaps, he just needs a little more time to process your news.

There are men who would feel like they had just won the lottery with such a revelation from their girlfriends. I know I will burst a few male bubbles when I say that having a bisexual girlfriend does not guarantee that she will want a ménage à trois. I recall that once a friend of mine with a bisexual wife asked her for a threesome. She agreed to his offer, provided the extra person was a man. My friend immediately turned down his wife's offer and never asked for a threesome again.

I would make it clear to your boyfriend that you are committed to this relationship. Regardless of your sexuality, no one wants a partner who is constantly accusing you of being unfaithful when it isn't true. Give him the choice to either trust you or part ways.

"Le jardinier peut décider de ce qui convient aux carottes,
mais nul ne peut choisir le bien des autres à leur place."
— Jean Paul Sartre

"The gardener can decide what is suitable for carrots, but no one can choose the good of others for them."

Letter 22

My boyfriend is a terrible cook. I love that he tries to help in the kitchen but most of his dishes are inedible. I don't want to hurt his feelings. Are French men as good in the kitchen as they seem to be in bed? Do you have any suggestions?

Bonita
Stamford, CT

Dear Bonita,

You are a *femme chanceuse*, a fortunate woman. Men are often accused of not helping around the house, especially in the kitchen. With a boyfriend who is willing to cook, you have won half the battle. Nobody is born a cook. It is a skill that is learned. Maybe your boyfriend could use your assistance. Perhaps, you could read recipes aloud for your boyfriend while he is cooking as a way to ensure he is following the directions correctly. Is he cooking in a hurry? Preparing a meal can be a slow process that requires patience.

One of my fondest customs in French culture is our use of food to bring families together. It does not begin when we sit down at the table. It begins with the selection of the ingredients at the market, continues with preparation in the kitchen, and the final leg of the journey takes us to the dining room table. Preparing a meal together can be an intimate experience for a couple. Consider taking a cooking class together. Great cooking in the kitchen leads to even greater cooking in the bedroom.

"En faisant l'amour comme en cuisine, ce qui est vite fait est mal fait." — French Proverb

"In making love as in cooking, what is done quickly is done badly."

Letter 23

How do you know when a guy is the one you want to spend the rest of your life with?

Monica
Helena, MT

Dear Monica,

You will know he is the one when he speaks of the future in terms of *we* and not *I*. You will know when you feel safe and content in his presence, not that you *need* him, but you *want* him around. You will know when he values your opinion without judgment. You will know when he supports your dreams and encourages you to be your own person. You will know when he listens to you with his ears, head, heart, and soul.

If you need him around and cannot live without him, this probably isn't the time to make important decisions about your future together. Relationships come with no guarantees, but I believe the odds are in your favor when you avoid fast, impulsive decisions. Don't get me wrong. You might know immediately after meeting someone that they are the perfect person for you. I am suggesting that you take time to get to know one another on a deeper level. If he is the right one, he isn't going anywhere.

"Une femme a besoin d'un homme qui la protège comme sa fille, qui l'aime comme sa femme et qui la respecte comme sa mère." — French Proverb

"A woman needs a man who protects her like his daughter, who loves her like his wife, and who respects her like his mother."

Letter 24

I am 35 and my husband is 56. From the time we first met, he has spoiled me and given me everything my heart desires. He has taken me all over the world and given me a life that I never dreamed imaginable. My problem is that I feel I have fallen out of love with him. Even when we're in the same room, I feel completely alone. I feel like a terrible person for wanting a divorce because he has been wonderful to me. Should I stay in this relationship out of guilt?

Monique
San Diego, CA

Dear Monique,

Sometimes old pots do not necessarily cook the best food. The possibility of having your partner lose interest in you when you are 21 years her senior is a risk that comes with dating younger women. People grow and change with time and experience. I am sure you have grown and matured during your marriage, whereas your husband was likely already who he was going to be when he met you.

I cannot in good conscience suggest that you stick it out with your husband simply because he has been good to you. I would not wish a loveless marriage on anyone. Your husband took a gamble by courting a much younger woman. His gamble has paid off until now. Life is much too short to deprive yourself of the pursuit of love; your husband knows this well.

"Quand l'amour n'est pas réciproque, le feu de la tristesse brule et consomme le cœur petit à petit." –French Proverb

"When love is not reciprocal, the fire of sadness burns and consumes the heart little by little."

Letter 25

I work full time and my husband stays home. He spends his days growing vegetables, canning, beekeeping, and selling produce at the farmers market. People pass off insulting comments as jokes about my husband being lucky because he gets to stay home and play video games all day. Why do people have such a problem with a woman being the primary breadwinner in a relationship?

Cameron
Austin, TX

Dear Cameron,

The most important thing in a couple is harmony. You and your husband have distributed tasks in a manner that works for you. The people who are stuck in the belief that traditional roles for men and women are the only way to go will never approve of your arrangement. To them, any nonconventional partnership is gossip-worthy.

The reversal of traditional roles between men and women is a reality these days. Fortunately, men are no longer bound to be the hunters. Today, especially among young people, women are making as much money if not more than men.

At the end of the day, your opinion is the only one that matters. Your husband seems to carry his weight and you do not feel taken advantage of, so that is that. Let the gossipers know your relationship is not up for discussion.

"Observer sans juger est la plus haute forme d'intelligence humaine car il n'existe pas de venin pire s'occuper des affaires des autres." — Blaise

"To observe without judgment is the highest form of human intelligence, because there is no worse poison than to mind the affairs of others."

Letter 26

I'm having the best sex of my life with a married man who isn't my husband. He wants me to get divorced and be with him completely. I am worried that the passion will fizzle out if we are no longer sneaking around. Do you think it's possible to maintain the spark of an affair long-term?

Sophie
Miami, FL

Dear Sophie,

Part of the charm and appeal of your relationship is that you are both waiting to see each other. There is that buildup of anticipation until you meet again. The taste of forbidden fruit increases the intensity and heightens the passion. For whatever the reason, men tend to be more adventurous with mistresses than with their wives. Making love in unusual places gives lovemaking a different taste. At home, sex in the same bed and sometimes the same position gets boring.

Based on my personal experience, an affair does not stand the test of time. To divorce your husband and marry your lover will change the dynamic of the relationship. Consider this: If you could suddenly have sex with your lover any time of day or night you desired, do you think you would maintain the intensity you both have right now? Yes, I suppose it is possible but not very likely. Also, when your lover is working late or out with his friends, will you worry that he is having an affair? Think this decision over carefully, especially if sex is the only thing that you and your lover have in common.

"Un couple n'est vraiment qu'un couple que s'il transpire au lit." — Frederic Dard

"A couple is really only a couple if they sweat in bed."

Letter 27

My husband brags about his skills in the bedroom but those skills only last about five to 10 minutes. How do you suggest I address this problem? I truly don't want to hurt his feelings.

Elena
Miami, FL

Dear Elena,

You chose your partner for reasons that only you know. I've heard women say that men who brag about their sexual prowess are usually bad in bed. Immaturity or insecurity aside, the discussion you need to have with your husband will sting a little. There's no way around it. A slightly bruised ego is inevitable, but your husband needs to know the error of his ways and, as his wife, you deserve to be sexually satisfied. Be loving, honest, and supportive with your words.

But don't stop there. Once you are both ready to get back on the horse, continue to be vocal. Give him instructions. Just because a man does not like to ask for directions doesn't mean that he won't accept directions when they are given to him. Most men will say that they would rather have a woman tell them what she wants than have them guess at what gets her off. After some intentional changes and a little practice, your husband may realize that there is no need to brag when his moves can do all of the talking for him.

"Les promesses de la nuit sont faites de beurre et fondent au soleil." — French Proverb

"The promises of the night are made of butter and melt in the sun."

Letter 28

None of my family or friends know I am bisexual. I have recently met a woman with whom I am very interested in pursuing a relationship, and I feel it is time that I stop living in the closet. How would you compare America to France? Is the French culture more accepting of the LGBTQ community than American culture is?

Tamara
Sumiton, AL

Dear Tamara,

Both France and America have places that are more progressive than others. While France has many conservative towns, Paris continues to be the city of tolerance. If you ever find yourself visiting Paris, be sure to make your way to the neighborhood called Le Marais, where the gay scene is central. In the chic Le Marais, it isn't unusual to see gay couples openly engaging in PDA without anyone batting an eyelash. There are multiple gay-friendly bars, clubs, and restaurants for the full (gay) Paris experience. In Paris overall, love is love.

Living in the Bible Belt state of North Carolina as I do, it is no surprise that the number of gay-friendly venues decreases. They exist but not in the quantities you will find in places like Paris, San Francisco, or New York City. I wish you the best of luck and I hope your family and friends receive your secret with love and acceptance.

"La personne bisexuelle a deux fois plus de chances le samedi soir." — Blaise

"A bisexual person has twice as many chances for love on a Saturday night."

Letter 29

My husband is no longer interested in sex. What should I do?

Hope
Baldwin City, KS

Dear Hope,

Lack of libido is a reality of life. Sex drives are high when men are younger and lower as they get older. Women seem to be the opposite. It reminds me of the letter *S*. Women's sexuality starts at the bottom, men's sexuality at the top, and both go in opposite directions. This explains why so many women become cougars. Their sexual peak is more in line with the drive of younger men.

You do not mention whether this lack of interest in sex was a gradual progression or something that happened suddenly. If this was a sudden change, I suggest ruling out any medical conditions. Is your husband taking any medications? There are medicines that lower your sex drive as a side effect. If that's not possible in your husband's case, I'll just go ahead and ask. Is there any possibility that your husband is wearing himself out in someone else's bed? Perhaps, that's something to consider.

I asked one of my most outspoken friends how she turns her husband on when she is in the mood and he is not. She told me her back massages never fail. While her man is enjoying a nice shoulder rub, she slips in an ear nibble and a few soft kisses on his neck to seal the deal. Occasionally, she will surprise him with porn. She said watching porn together always leads to sex.

Ultimately, no amount of coaxing on your part will work without a willing participant. Your husband has to want to get out of his funk and put in some effort.

"Des paroles carrées n'entrent pas dans des oreilles rondes."
— French Proverb

"Square words do not fit into round ears."

Letter 30

All my life, I have struggled with weight. Can you tell me the secrets of French women? Au revoir!

Olivia
New Haven, CT

Dear Olivia,

Americans seem to be fascinated by the French lifestyle. You can cross France from Normandy to the French Riviera and you will not find a French secret to staying slim. It is a myth. I see it more as that universal mindset by French women to associate beauty with body size. They have amazing self-control and often know how to find the right balance between *la joie de vivre* and staying fit.

Culturally, the French tend to eat their meals at specific times, and snacking between meals is more of an American custom. In general, the French also do more walking than Americans. If you consider less food intake with more exercise a secret, there you have it. That is how French women stay fit. This doesn't mean that every woman has a perfect BMI in France. In a study done in 2014, 42 percent of French women between the ages of 35 and 44 were overweight. We all know the benefits of maintaining a healthy weight, but a woman with a few extra pounds is still beautiful in my eyes. Weight should not define beauty. The key to losing weight is sensibility, not some secret found in France.

"Le poids ne doit pas être une limite pour faire ce que l'on aime. C'est une infime partie de vous."— French Proverb

"The weight should not be a limit to doing what you love. It's a tiny part of you."

Letter 31

Do French men base their sexual ideas on unrealistic porn like so many American men do?

Eleonor
Ecorse, MI

Dear Eleonor,

According to Pornhub, France is the sixth largest consumer of porn in the world. Despite sex education taught in France, pornography remains an alternative sexuality educator for men. A survey done by the French agency IFOP states that almost one in two French men have tried to reproduce positions or scenes seen in porn movies. Ultimately, men are men, regardless of their nationalities.

I see nothing wrong with watching porn alone or as a couple. Like alcohol, porn should be consumed with moderation. For some couples, it can be a fun way to initiate foreplay. Of course, it is not everyone's cup of tea. A friend of mine told me she could never take it seriously. When she watched porn with her lover, she scoffed most of the time. Whether it's the overly dramatic moans or the occasional camera glances, she has yet to see a porn video that gets her motor running. However, when her man has been an extra good boy, she will blow him while he is watching his favorite porn. Her words, not mine!

"Pour la pornographie, les hommes Français et Américains sont du tabac de la même pipe." — French Proverb

"Regarding pornography, French and American men are tobacco from the same pipe."

Letter 32

After many failed relationships, I have decided to be celibate for a while. I want to examine my previous choices and reset my selection process. Do you think removing my sexual needs from the table will help me do this?

Carla
Minneapolis, MN

Dear Carla,

I respect your decision to take a break. Contrary to what many men believe, sex is not oxygen. We can live without it for as long as we wish. Your decision makes me think of an alcoholic deciding to quit drinking. I am not suggesting sex is bad but sometimes we let sex lead us to people who are not a good fit for us. In those circumstances, sex is a drug.

I think you have the right idea. It always concerns me when a woman says she has never spent time alone without being in a relationship, or worse, that she can't be without one. Taking a time-out from dating will help you focus all of your attention on yourself. Reflect on past relationships but do not dwell on them for too long. What makes a bad relationship a tragedy is when we do not use it as a learning experience for the next one.

"Un livre qu'on quitte sans en avoir extrait quelque chose est un livre qu'on a pas lu." —French Proverb

"A book you leave without extracting something from, it is a book you haven't read."

Letter 33

Are French people more inclined to be into BDSM?

Carol
Seattle, WA

Dear Carol,

I cannot speak to the exact numbers or how the French compare to other nationalities regarding BDSM, but I can tell you that there is no shortage of BDSM venues in France. Whatever your fetish, there is a place for you.

Bondage and Discipline, Domination and Submission, Sadism and Masochism, more commonly known as BDSM, is the theme of many clubs found in most big cities in France. Paris, the city I love, has multiple BDSM clubs. Swingers also have their pick of venues. Dominant women and their submissives have a club all to themselves where the men must leave their ego at the door.

Most of the BDSM clubs in France are private clubs and extremely discreet for obvious reasons. Don't forget to bring your safe word.

"A chacun ses gouts." — *French Proverb*

"Everyone to his/her own tastes."

Letter 34

I want to know if Frenchmen are like American men in bed. Sex with my boyfriend is over when he orgasms, even if I haven't.

Katie
Reno, NV

Dear Katie,

The sex toy industry would love your boyfriend. The more men suck in bed, the greater the demand for sex toys. Your question is not a matter of nationality. Many men are just selfish.

Between American and French men, I would say that French men have an edge in this department. They believe that their partner's pleasure is very important, and they tend to make more of an effort to learn about and invest in knowing a woman's anatomy. French women are the reason. French women are very outspoken and have little patience for selfish lovers. If one is not getting the job done, he will hear about it. He may also be replaced. French men are motivated to be good in bed by the desire to avoid the stinging disappointment of a vocal French woman.

Your boyfriend has a few improvements to make. I compare sex to cooking. Each meal has its own special list of ingredients and instructions. Women are unique individuals with unique needs. One lover may want hard and aggressive sex while another prefers it slow and steady. A good lover takes the time to learn what their partner needs and makes an effort to satisfy. A penis is like a muscle that requires practice and focus to keep under control. A man who values his lover will take the time to master his own organ. Katie, be vocal about what you need from your boyfriend. You owe it to yourself. He may not like hearing it, but he will soon appreciate how much better the sex becomes when you are both satisfied at the end.

"Tout muscle qui travaille se développe." — *French Proverb*

"Any muscle, [including a penis], takes practice to make
it work well."

Letter 35

While using my dad's phone, I discovered that he is cheating on my mother. The only person I have told is my boyfriend, and he thinks I should stay out of it. I can't imagine keeping such a secret from my mother. I'm just wondering if I should confront my father, tell my mother, or speak to both of them at the same time. This feels like a nightmare. What should I do?

Tania
Raleigh, NC

Dear Tania,

That is a heavy secret to carry as a daughter. I would encourage you to tell your mother privately.

It is up to her to decide what to do with the information. I am reminded of a situation where a family's adult children were shocked to learn about their father's infidelity but were even more shocked to discover that the mother knew of the other relationship all along. If I were in your mother's shoes, I would prefer a bitter truth to a sugary lie.

"Même si la vérité peut être douloureuse parfois, elle blesse toujours moins que le mensonge à long terme."
— *French Proverb*

"Even if the truth can be painful sometimes, it always hurts less than a long-term lie."

Letter 36

My husband's masturbating gets on my nerves. I hate it...I feel like I am not enough for him. Does this mean that I don't satisfy him?

Tonya
Washington, DC

Dear Tonya,

No, and I don't think you should panic. Many men with high sex drives use masturbation to relieve sexual tension. Sometimes the wife is unavailable, and other times, it is just easier to sit back, watch some porn, and knock one out. Now, if your husband is preoccupied with masturbation to the point where it affects his work or your sex life, then I would be concerned. Men have multiple sexual thoughts and erections throughout the day. Masturbation is a normal and healthy activity for all genders.

"Le sexe masculin est ce qu'il y a de plus léger au monde, une simple pensée le soulève." —Frédéric Dard

"A cock is the lightest thing in the world; a simple thought raises it."

Letter 37

How does a Frenchman make love to a woman?

Loretta
Paris, TX

Dear Loretta,

I am not a spokesman for all French men, but I am willing to share details about my personal style. I do differentiate between sex and lovemaking. Sometimes sex is sex, and other times sex is part of making love. To be clear, whether I am fucking or making love is decided by my lover, not by me. She makes that call. Your question is about making love so I will keep my focus there.

Making love to a woman starts long before we are in the same room. French men are big on romance and expressions of love. We bring flowers or a favorite dessert to our lover's place of work for no reason other than to let her know that we were thinking of her. If you have been on the streets of France, you can see these expressions of love everywhere.

Contrary to what many men believe, pounding into a woman like a mechanical rabbit is not impressive. I am not knocking the pounding, but I am saying that there are many other moves to lovemaking; pounding a woman against the shower wall is only one move out of many. I like to be proactive by making my partner feel comfortable prior to our encounter. The typical American romantic dinner is nice but not mandatory. Sometimes a thoughtful gesture touches a woman's heart more effectively than going to a restaurant every time. Preliminaries are very important. I would never bother taking shortcuts. Lovemaking is like a beautiful ballroom dance; every step is as important as the last.

It is a monumental mistake for a man to think his style is universal and will make every woman happy. Women are unique; a smart lover will do his homework. He will put in the effort to get to know a woman and find out what turns her on. A man who uses the same moves on all of his lovers should never expect universal results. Lovemaking is about touching, kissing, and slowly building up to penetration. I enjoy taking control of everything prior to and after lovemaking. Making love does not stop after orgasms and a man should avoid leaving the bed quickly or rolling over and falling asleep. In fact, some of my best conversations with my lovers have happened after sex.

Describing what I do with a lover feels like bragging, so I decided to ask someone very special to describe her experience with me. This was our conversation:

Blaise: "I want you to describe me as a lover."

Brenda: "Why?"

Blaise: "For my new book."

Brenda: "You're going to share that with the world?"

Blaise: "Not with the world, with my readers."

Brenda: "Should I say all of it?"

Blaise: "Whatever you feel comfortable sharing."

Brenda: "If you're sure about this, here goes. Blaise is very romantic. He checks in with me at least a couple of times a day, asking how I am and, of course, flirting with me. He is very clear about what he wants and makes sure I want the same thing. He asks me if he can 'take me' before we meet. If I decline, he will ask if I prefer to do something else. This makes me feel like he wants to spend time with me as a person and not that he only wants to get laid.

"When he arrives at my house, he says 'bonjour' and he finds it hard not to touch me or kiss me immediately. He always wants to know how I am. We go upstairs and undress. But, unlike a typical American man, we don't do anything sexual right away. Instead, we talk, caress, kiss, flirt, and hold each other close, as though we can't get close enough. He strokes my hair and caresses my back; he tells me how beautiful I am and how much he has been thinking about being with me. Sometimes we talk about private, emotional feelings we've had during the day. Other times we talk about current events or something funny that happened to us.

"Blaise loves having his cock sucked, and I love sucking it. The more I suck, the wetter I get. I could go on for a long time but he often stops me and has to take me. I've had a few lovers, not a ton, but enough. Blaise is very inventive. He thinks of different ways to have sex. He takes his time, which I love. He is not in a hurry. It's all about pleasuring me. He often changes my position and takes me again until I have earth-shattering orgasm after orgasm. Blaise makes me feel like he gets all of his pleasure from pleasing me. He is not a selfish lover like I have had in the past. I have to have music going when he comes over because I'm afraid I'll disturb the neighbors.

"I enjoy the next stage of our lovemaking almost as much. Blaise likes to stay inside of me, to stay close, so we remain intertwined and we lie there listening to each other breathe, enjoying how our bodies are reacting to each other. He doesn't make excuses to get dressed and leave. Blaise takes me in his arms again, strokes my hair, caresses me, and we talk about our lovemaking. I'm a giggler, so often I'll laugh and giggle while we talk about what we've done and what we'll do next. Then we do it all over againand again."

"Faire l'amour est un plaisir, un appétit, un besoin, un amusement, et non pas un devoir." —*Ninon de Lenclos*

"Making love is a pleasure, an appetite, a need. It is joy, not a duty."

Letter 38

My boyfriend is obsessed with nipples. He even downloads nipple porn. Should I suggest he seeks professional help?

Tammy
Richmond, VA

Dear Tammy,

   Nipples and breasts are like fingers of the same hand. To men, they represent femininity and sensuality. We are bombarded by ads and magazine covers with breasts everywhere we look. Your boyfriend cannot escape that reality. The most important question to ask yourself is whether his nipple obsession is affecting his ability to be a good boyfriend and a productive citizen. Is he skipping work to watch nipple porn? Is his fascination taking precedence over your needs? If so, then he may need to seek help. If not, try using his obsession to your advantage. Nipples are erogenous zones with many sensitive nerve endings. They can be pulled, twisted, rubbed, and bitten into orgasm.

Consider turning the tables on him. So many women ignore the opportunity to pleasure their man through his nipples. It is a nice surprise to see a woman show love to a body part other than the dick. Those nerve endings are not exclusive to women.

"Les seins d'une femme ne sont pas des saints, mais ils ont un pouvoir magique." — Dian Diallo

"A woman's breasts are not saints, but they have magical power."

Letter 39

My husband is so stingy that he infuriates me when we argue about spending money. I understand that having a nest egg is important but being able to enjoy life and have experiences while we still can should be important too. What is your perspective on finances within a relationship?

Madison
Salt Lake City, UT

Dear Madison,

Without knowing what your husband does that drives you crazy, it is hard to give you my perspective. Is he stingy because he has money to buy a new car but keeps driving the family around in an old one with a busted air conditioner? Or is he stingy because he won't agree to your tenth pair of Manolo Blahniks and your fifth Michael Kors bag?

There is a difference between stingy and frugal. A frugal person is careful with expenses. They research purchases and make sure they are getting their money's worth. A stingy person is someone who will go out of their way not to spend money on anyone, including themselves. They may intentionally load up on the complimentary bread at a restaurant and then decide not to order a meal. Growing up in poverty, without always having food in the refrigerator, is one reason why some people are more likely to be frugal with their money, for fear of experiencing those difficult times again. Is that a possible factor? Ironically, many of us tend to pair up with a partner with opposite views on money. There is usually a spender and a saver in a relationship. While this can be annoying at times, it is great for checks and balances.

Stinginess is a bad thing; being frugal is not. I would suggest you not ask your husband's opinion when something essential is needed; just buy it. Be honest with yourself. The difference between *wants* and *needs* is everything.

> *"Un avare se suicide avec un revolver acheté au marché aux puces."* — *Max Jacob*
>
> "A miser commits suicide with a gun bought at the flea market."

Letter 40

My husband and I have been trying to conceive for six years without success. I have been tested and everything seems to be fine. My husband, however, refuses to get tested. I am considering walking away from this marriage because I have always wanted to have a child. Am I being selfish?

Grace
Louisville, Kentucky

Dear Grace,

Your story reminds me of my childhood friend, Michaud, who married a German man. They tried to have children together for years. Michaud blamed herself and her husband figured his wife just could not conceive. After their divorce, Michaud got pregnant by her new man within the first year.

Not all couples are lucky enough to have a child naturally. Infertility is not just a woman's issue. Sadly, some men believe their in-

LOVE LIKE THE FRENCH

ability to have children is directly connected to their masculinity. In contrast, I know of a man who had a vasectomy before getting married and kept it a secret from his wife.

The part of your question that stands out to me is where you say, "He refuses to get tested." Your husband must know how important this is to you but he is not willing to do everything possible to make your dream a reality. This leaves me wondering if he is as enthusiastic about having children as you are. Perhaps, he does not want children but doesn't know how to tell you.

Your situation is serious enough to deserve a serious conversation with your husband. He should know that you are willing to walk away from the relationship since he does not appear to share your dream. I do not think it is selfish to want children of your own. As a father, I can tell you that raising children is not always easy but it is the most rewarding job in the world.

"Etre parent est l'un des emplois le plus difficiles sur terre. Beaucoup d'hommes sont te terrorisés par les couches."
— Blaise

"Parenting is one of the toughest jobs on earth. Many men are terrorized by diapers."

Letter 41

How do I make my fiancé stop complaining when I don't want to have sex with him? He wants it every day; I do not.

Helen
Alamo, NV

Dear Helen,

I'm wondering if you give your fiancé specific reasons for turning him down or if you say you are not in the mood each time. Are you extremely tired at the end of the day? Is there something he could do to alleviate your exhaustion? Perhaps, by helping more around the house? As a man, it is hard for me to say that your husband is being insensitive for wanting for make love to his fiancée. Sometimes partners just have vastly different sex drives. Perhaps, you two would benefit from a few sessions of couple's therapy to find a middle ground. The odds of your problem resolving itself after marriage are slim and sex should never feel like a chore to either gender.

"Une femme accro au sexe, on l'appelle une nymphomane.
Alors qu'un homme accro au sexe, on l'appelle…un homme."
— Foozine

"When a woman is addicted to sex, she is called a
nymphomaniac. While when a man is addicted to sex, we call
him…a man."

Letter 42

My boyfriend is friends with all of his exes on social media. Am I being unreasonable to expect him to cut ties with past relationships?

Rosalie
Irving, TX

Dear Rosalie,

I believe staying in touch with your ex is disrespectful to your current partner. An ex is not just a friend. An ex is someone with whom you shared an emotional bond. An ex has intimate knowledge of you. No matter how hard you try to convince your new lover that there is nothing going on between you and your ex, they will always be made to feel uncomfortable at the thought of you two still communicating. I would not flaunt my exes in front of a current lover and expect her to be okay with it.

My friend, Gabrielle, has experience on this topic from the perspective of the ex. Here's our discussion:

Blaise: "You remain in contact with many of your exes?"

Gabrielle: "With a few of them, yes. "

Blaise: "Why?"

Gabrielle: "Several reasons. One reason is that they asked me not to cut ties with them. One of them pleaded with me not to stop communication. He said he couldn't imagine his life without me in it. But the main reason is that we developed a friendship before we started dating so we still had that bond. No one wants to lose a friend. I knew I would never sleep with them while they were in new relationships so I was comfortable not ending our friendships."

Blaise: "Did you ever talk to your exes about intimate things while they were in new relationships?"

Gabrielle: "Of course. Men like to reminisce about good times. I expect them to bring up the past. We can reminisce for a minute but then I have to pump the brakes on the conversation."

Blaise: "Why do you change the subject?"

Gabrielle: "Because I know where the conversation will lead, and I'm not interested in going there."

Blaise: "Where will the conversation lead?"

Gabrielle: "It leads to cheating."

Blaise: "Are you sure that's what they want?"

Gabrielle: "Of course, it is. I know these men pretty well."

Blaise: "Do they tell their current partners about you?"

Gabrielle: "Sometimes they do, but they leave out a lot of details. Sometimes they can't mention me, and I am kept a secret."

Blaise: "Do you think a man is being disrespectful to his partner when he maintains communication with an ex?"

Gabrielle: "I do, because even though he might not be sleeping with the ex, the emotional bond between them continues to be reinforced as long as they are communicating. If their current partners were listening in on our conversations, they would not like some of what was said."

Blaise: "Give me an example of one of those conversations."

Gabrielle: "One of my exes was getting married. He convinced his fiancée that I was one of his best friends in order for her to be okay with our friendship. He invited me to the wedding."

Blaise: "Why would his fiancée agree to have you at the wedding?"

Gabrielle: "He told her we never dated, we never had sex, and that I was like a sister to him."

Blaise: "Did you go to the wedding?"

Gabrielle: "I didn't go. He said it was the most important day of his life and he needed me to be a part of it, but as a woman, I knew how I would feel to find out the truth if I were in his fiancée's shoes."

Blaise: "How would you have felt as the fiancée?"

Gabrielle: "I would have killed him for making a fool of me on my wedding day. He didn't have enough sense to do the right thing by her, but I did."

Blaise: "Did you really not go to the wedding for her sake or was it for yours?"

Gabrielle: "Most definitely for her sake. I ended the relationship. I wanted him to move on and be in a good place. He had trouble cutting the strings."

Blaise: "If you wanted to continue a sexual relationship with your exes while they were in new relationships, would that be possible?"

Gabrielle: *laughs* "You're kidding, right? Yes, of course. Sex with an ex is always possible. That would have been the ideal scenario for them, not for me."

"Retourner vers un ex, c'est comme reprendre le Titanic en espérant qu'il ne coulera pas." —Blaise

"Going back to an ex is like reboarding the Titanic hoping it won't sink."

Letter 43

I am dating a man who has a hard time expressing his love. How do I get him to understand that romance should not be confined to the bedroom?

Barbara
North Charleston, SC

Dear Barbara,

Romance does not begin and end in the bedroom. A man should not expect to ignore a woman all day and then turn on the charm when he climbs into bed. Romance does not seem to be a big part of American culture the way it is in France. Walk through the streets of Paris for a day and you will notice gestures of romance everywhere and not just on Valentine's Day.

Not all men are comfortable being emotionally naked. To be romantic means to put yourself out there. I notice men walking side by side with their partners and not making physical contact.

French men will kiss their wives on the lips in public without hesitation. American culture seems more accepting of guns than of sexuality. I recall seeing an affectionate couple at a sporting event some time ago and someone yelling, "Get a room!" I cannot imagine anything like that ever happening in France. Seeing people in love is a beautiful sight to the French. We are not offended by expressions of love. I was married to a woman who often traveled for business. Our embraces, our kisses, and our hand-holding would draw a lot of attention, even in airports, where people are expected to be emotional about seeing a loved one leave town.

I suggest that your partner learn your hobbies and interests. Romance can be something as simple as a surprise text in the middle of the day with a quote out of your favorite book. It can be a single rose left on your car's windshield. I am not suggesting a man has to kiss his wife's feet every day, but I am saying that intimacy in the form of thoughtfulness and dialogue with clothes on is an important part of the process that leads to the bedroom.

"La véritable intimité est celle qui permet de rêver ensemble avec des rêves différentes." —Jacques Salome

"True intimacy is that which allows us to dream together with different dreams."

Letter 44

My fiancé promised me that we would be married by now but
he keeps postponing the wedding. We have been engaged for five
years. I feel like he's stringing me along. Should I give him an
ultimatum?

Faith
Mesa, AZ

Dear Faith,

It is rare for anyone to think that an ultimatum is a good idea. In
your case, however, the suggestion has its merits. I don't know your
fiancé, but sometimes people are hesitant to change things they believe do not need changing. It is possible he is of the mindset *if it isn't
broken, don't fix it.* There seems to be a contradiction in views when it
comes to marriage. One camp believes that marriage is just a piece of
paper that has no bearing on a relationship, while the other camp believes that relationships go downhill the minute a couple says, "I do."

It is time for an honest discussion with your fiancé. If not getting married is a dealbreaker for you, then an ultimatum seems reasonable. But consider this: Do you really want to marry someone who is marrying you because of an ultimatum? Five years is more than enough time for anyone to know how they feel about a partner. I believe his postponements are sending a message. I hope you can find some common ground and remember that giving an ultimatum means you must be willing to say goodbye.

"Le temps fuit, et le temps perdu ne revient jamais."
— *Pierre Veron*

"Time flies, and lost time never comes back."

Letter 45

When I was in France, I noticed a great deal of PDA in French culture. Why do you think Americans aren't as comfortable with PDA?

Tiffany
Pittsburgh, PA

Dear Tiffany,

I have had that same question in my mind for years. I have observed in America that public displays of affection are reserved for children but rarely for couples. I do believe that couples in America save feelings and affection for the bedroom only. In France, men are proud to spotlight their women publicly. Making a physical connection with one's lover is seen as chivalrous. If Americans believe that foreplay prior to sex starts only in the bedroom, it is a huge mistake. There is no shame in showing the world your sentiments. Is it the lack of sex education or the Puritan mindset at play? You certainly saw on the French metro that men love tapping their partners' butts or kissing passionately. French women love that. It is also a signal that a man has a plan on his mind. I am not an ornithologist, I never studied birds, but if you look at the French male's approach toward women, you will see similarities between French men and birds. A woman is reassured when a man claims her publicly and the message is not ambiguous.

The lack of PDA in America is a message that a woman needs to pay attention to. A couple in love should be comfortable acknowledging each other publicly. Sometimes a man who is unwilling to show affection in public is intentionally leaving his options open. He does not want attractive single women to know he is in a relationship. Those who love their partner should know that words are not enough. A simple touch, holding hands, or a kiss are the true "measure" of love. I smile when I read that men are *visual* and women are *mental*; it seems backward. If men were more visual, then they would be more demonstrative of public affection. It is absurd to me when celebrities showing PDA make the news. For the French, kissing is cultural and is not reserved for the famous. Why save the kisses for the bedroom? Life is short. Couples in America should stop acting like strangers in public. Since Americans love France, why not imitate the French and show the world that you are in love?

"L'éloge le plus grand c'est l'imitation." — **French Proverb**

"The greatest praise is imitation."

Letter 46

I seem to attract men without stability and I always find myself supporting the relationship financially. Why do I attract this type of man?

Elisa
Ashley, OH

Dear Elisa,

I do not know why you attract this type of man, but the real question is what you do after you've attracted one. Are you allowing yourself to support a man for the sake of being in a relationship? Is that the type of man you feel you deserve? Who we (both men and women) attract has everything to do with our self-worth. Our self-worth determines our standards. Reflect on what is important to you and set your standards. Then do not allow anyone to talk you into compromising on those standards once they are set. Sometimes it is better to be alone than to be in bad company.

"Qui se marie fait bien, qui reste célibataire fait mieux."
— French Proverb

"Who gets married does well, who stays single does better."

Letter 47

My boyfriend refuses to kiss me after I please him orally. It's insulting. Do French men kiss their partners on the mouth after oral sex?

Tiana
Athens, GA

Dear Tiana,

I cannot speak on behalf of all French men but I have never heard anyone in my circle complain about kissing his lover on the lips after oral sex. Brushing one's teeth between blow jobs is stupidity and a big turnoff. Any man who refuses to kiss a woman after she has done something so intimate with him is being disrespectful. If sperm were toxic, the first to die from it would be the man himself. It is an act of selfishness to refuse your lover's lips.

My friend Alexandria described it like this:

"A slow kiss on my lips while they are still glistening with your cum is a compliment to me and the ultimate show of gratitude. If you ever refuse to kiss my lips after I suck your dick, that will be the last time you feel these lips on that dick."

"L'égoïsme est ennemi du bonheur, il défend d'admirer et d'aimer." — French Proverb

"Selfishness is the enemy of happiness; it forbids admiring and loving."

Letter 48

My fiancé and I have decided to abide by our religious beliefs and abstain from sex before marriage. We have been dating for almost a year now. I am worried that, if I wait, I could end up married to someone who I'm not sexually compatible with. Am I making a mistake?

Adele
Salt Lake City, UT

Dear Adele,

I respect your decision to wait if your faith drives all of your decisions. Personally, I would never be willing to abide by such a rule. I can't imagine marrying someone without knowing if we are sexually compatible. Some skills can be learned but other issues might be acts of nature that are out of your control.

Few people wait for their wedding night. A friend once told me that some women will do everything sexual with their partner except vaginal penetration in order to say that they waited to marry before having sex. The abstinence loophole of the century! I am not suggesting you do this but at least take a peek under the hood to be sure you can work with the size of the engine.

"Ne sois pas trop dur avec toi même, sauf en cas d'érection."
— *French Proverb*

"Don't be too hard on yourself, except in case of an erection."

I struggle to comprehend the religious logic of waiting to get married before having sex. I barely survive the agony of the American dating waiting game, where women decide on a certain number of dates to wait before having sex. It is absurd. My record number of dates with the same woman without having sex is seven. I hated it. Don't misunderstand me, you should take your time. I support that. A woman should never feel pressured into having sex. Rather, I am referring to women who are feeling that sexual chemistry and want to have sex as much as I do but hold back because we have not reached the number of dates they decided we should wait. I blame American men and their double standards for this. I believe this is the real reason why so many American women feel they must wait. Men who sleep around are celebrated as bachelors and playboys but women who sleep around are stigmatized for the same behavior. French women would tell American men where to stick that double standard. When a French woman wants to have sex, she will do so without fear of being labeled. When she is ready, she is ready, and will offer no apologies. The decision to have sex is made during the date and not before. That type of confidence is immensely attractive.

Letter 49

My younger sister is 31 and very successful. She has a great career and owns a beautiful home. She is also a virgin and has never been in a relationship. Is it possible to be truly happy without a love life?

Amanda
Chesterfield, MO

Dear Amanda,

A smart woman will not seek a relationship merely because it is a social convention. Honestly, I applaud her for her accomplishments at that young an age. Clearly, having a relationship is not a priority for her at this time. It may never be. I believe that a person is capable of feeling fulfilled without romantic involvement, especially if they are career-driven and focused on success.

A single friend once said to me, "I'm not always in the mood to deal with men. Sometimes I just need to be on my own. Anyway, no man can give me orgasms harder than the ones I can give myself."

I do not think you should worry about your sister, nor try to solve what you perceive to be a problem. She seems to have her life under control.

"On ne prend pas les médicaments à la place du malade."
— *French Proverb*

"No one should take medicines on behalf of the patient."

Letter 50

My husband has been very unhappy with me ever since I gave birth to our first child. He keeps reminding me that I am still his wife and not just a mother. Is it normal for a man to feel jealousy toward his own child?

Odile
Antioch, TN

Dear Odile,

I couldn't tell you if it's normal but I can tell you it's unacceptable. I cannot imagine the added stress he is causing you by behaving this way. As if the worries of having a new baby aren't enough!

Perhaps, a therapist might validate his feelings of neglect but since I am not a therapist, I will say that he is acting very immature and needs to grow up. Did he forget he is a parent too? Does he not know that babies require a lot of attention? He should be supporting you at this time and doing whatever it takes to make motherhood easier for you.

What is he angry about? Is it his need for sex or his need for attention? He should know that the best gift he can give his baby is to love you. Having a baby is the one occasion when a husband has to take a back seat to the star of the show.

"Les bébés ont besoin de communication. Le lait et le sommeil ne suffisent pas." — Bernard Werber

"Babies need communication. Milk and sleep are not enough."

Letter 51

I am falling for a married man who I met online. Is it crazy to believe that he will leave his wife to be with me?

Anne
Martinsburg, WV

Dear Anne,

What has this man done so far to prove to you that he is divorcing his wife? Anything? I believe that if you only listen to his words and not his actions, you will go crazy. A married man feeling stuck in a rut meets an exciting new woman and has a whirlwind affair. It is a story older than time. I would encourage you to be observant of the way a man treats his wife and never expect him to treat his next wife any differently. I call this a *"Bonjour, Au-revoir"* relationship ("Hello, Goodbye"). They rarely last. If he did leave his wife, would you be able to trust that he won't cheat on you? My honest opinion: run.

"La plus grande lâcheté d'un homme est d'éveiller l'amour d'une femme...sans vraiment l'intention de l'aimer."
— Augusto Branco

"The great cowardice of a man is to awaken the love of a woman without really intending to love her."

Letter 52

I don't feel pleasure when I'm having sex. Does that mean I am asexual?

Betty
Charlotte, NC

Dear Betty,

I suggest you see a doctor about your concerns. It is difficult to speculate without knowing your circumstances. Do you love your partner? Is your partner attentive to your needs during sex? Is your partner simply a terrible lover? Are there other problems causing you stress that might affect your sex life? I can only speculate. My advice is to see a medical doctor first and, after receiving a clean bill of health, see a therapist. I believe it would be beneficial to explore your feelings with a professional.

"Ce n'est ni corps à corps que nous avons besoin mais d'un cœur à cœur." —Pierre Teilhard

"It's not body-to-body that we need, but heart-to-heart."

Letter 53

My ex posted naked pictures of me after finding out that I had gotten married. After I threatened to sue him, he took down the pictures, but my husband found out and is furious with both of us. How long should I let my husband punish me for a mistake that I made in the past?

Erica
Pittsburgh, PA

Dear Erica,

Everyone has a past. I don't think it is right to punish a spouse for indiscretions made prior to the relationship. I am not aware of any legal recourse you can take now that the pictures have been taken down. Unless your ex is making attempts to reach out to you, I would put this picture nightmare to rest. I can understand your husband feeling disappointed that this ever happened or maybe even embarrassment at the thought of your pictures being shared online. Perhaps, your husband is open to therapy as a couple. He could probably use some reassurance that this behavior will never happen again.

"Ne te noie pas dans le passé, nul ne peut le changer." —
French Proverb

"Don't drown in the past; no one can change it."

Letter 54

My boyfriend won't compromise about sex. He gets upset when I complain because he can't get me off but I need more foreplay and I've told him that. His idea of foreplay is getting oral. I hate that. Have you heard similar complaints from other women? How do I get my boyfriend to pay attention to my needs?

Carole
Fayetteville, AR

Dear Carole,

Your question is a tough one. It is hard to respond to this from a male perspective. I do not think that even the greatest male psychologists can feel what is going on in the minds of women during sex. I passed your question to one of the most transparent women I know when it comes to sex, my friend, Geneviève. She has been married three times and is never shy about discussions on this topic. Here is her answer:

"Dear Blaise,

When it comes to sex, women are not wired like men. I can speak for myself and I know many of my friends can relate to what I am going to say. A woman's orgasm is mostly mental. When I am having sex, all sorts of thoughts, not always about sex, cross my mind, especially during penetration or when a partner is going down on me. I might be thinking, *I am not feeling anything, this is gross, I don't want him down there, it is taking too long, I wonder if he really enjoys licking pussy, it's starting to feel good but it will take me a long time to come.* It can be a lot of pressure.

"Most women take longer to orgasm for the same reason. We let our thoughts and insecurities take over during sex. We get self-conscious. That's why foreplay is very important. Talking about what we want, touching, and kissing before getting into it is so important. A partner must get the woman excited to increase the blood flow to the pussy. I must feel good during foreplay until I'm tready for more. I am very visual. I want to see the penetration. I taught my husband to do the things that work best for me. Now we make great love together. We have become phenomenal partners.

"You asked whether or not my husband pays attention to my needs in bed. Yes, but even so, if he keeps pounding my pussy over and over, it becomes numb. *C'est un tue-l'amour* ("It's a passion killer"). Due to continuous friction, the friction numbs my clit and after a while it is hard to orgasm again. I prefer my husband to alternate between eating me out and penetration. That is the way it is best for me and I can't explain it. Sometimes the winning technique is to fuck awhile and then get eaten out, especially after my husband has fucked me from behind.

"Our clits are like men's penises. Just like an irritated penis will not perform well, an irritated clit won't either. A woman's thinking is hard for a man to comprehend; if the woman doesn't want an orgasm, she is not going to have one. It's all mental.

"It is also very important for me that I am sexually attracted to my partner's scent. My husband and I love to smell each other during sex. I do believe that there is a connection between smell and attraction.

"I have met all kinds of guys in my life. Often, *un bon coup* ("a good fuck") is not good at eating pussy. It is like someone with a gun shooting and always missing the target. I would say that it is important to get a woman off first because once the man gets off, he's usually done and is no longer able to focus on pleasing the woman.

"I personally encourage women to use toys. They help us get comfortable with our bodies, and sex toys do not have time limitations. When a woman is comfortable with her partner, she learns what he enjoys doing and that takes off the pressure of wondering whether or not he is enjoying a particular act. It is liberating; it releases the performance pressure. You know, some women are very shy about talking about what they like because it is embarrassing.

"I hope my experiences will be helpful for Carole. Make sure to tell her that she should explain sex to her boyfriend by comparing it to an oven. The oven needs to be preheated before putting a pizza inside. If the oven is not warm enough, the pizza won't cook. Foreplay is the time spent preheating that oven. It is important for great sex."

"L'amour sans préliminaires c'est comme une pizza sans fromage." **— French Proverb**

"Love without foreplay is like a pizza without cheese."

Letter 55

My boyfriend of three years says marriage is just a piece of paper. I was brought up to believe that marriage is the ultimate relationship goal. How do the French view marriage?

Yolanda
Auburn, WA

Dear Yolanda,

If marriage is so important to you, then you are wasting your precious time. You cannot make your boyfriend marry you nor should you want to marry someone who is doing it to appease your wishes. Marriage does not come with guarantees but to many it is an important symbol of commitment. Marriage also comes with legal benefits that a boyfriend/girlfriend relationship does not offer. You two are going to need to have a serious discussion to make some decisions about your future.

"Un bon, honnête et franc concubinage, vaut souvent mieux qu'un mauvais mariage." — **French Proverb**

"A good, honest, and frank cohabitation is often better than a bad marriage."

Letter 56

I have been cheated on. I am extremely hurt and angry. My partner feels horrible about what he did and has repeatedly told me he's sorry. When I tell him that I need time to think things over, he cries and promises that it will never happen again. I love him but I don't know that I can ever trust him again. Is a cheater always a cheater?

Monica
Virginia Beach, VA

Dear Monica,

"Once a cheater, always a cheater" is a common response to infidelity. While it is easy to write off all cheaters with that popular phrase, the truth is that people are indeed capable of having an affair, feeling remorseful, and never repeating that mistake again. You probably want to know how that is possible and how you can know if your partner is one of those people.

I wish I could tell you with certainty that your partner is capable of this but you know I can't. What I do know is that someone who seeks to learn the reasons behind their infidelity is making an effort to make sure it never happens again. If your partner is offering excuses for his indiscretions or blaming his actions on something you did or did not do, then I would not hold out much hope of his affair being a one-time mistake.

If you choose to forgive him, do it because it is what you really want and not for any other reason. Staying in a toxic relationship for reasons such as the children or finances is a guaranteed recipe for disaster.

"Une faute avouée est à moitié pardonnée." — *French Proverb*

"A confessed fault is half forgiven."

Letter 57

I have been happily married for 15 years. Recently, I was seduced by a woman who I hired to do work in my home. I have never been with a woman or even been curious about being with one, but the truth is, this was the best sex I have ever had in my life. Do you think I was gay all along without knowing?

Miranda
Rochester, NY

Dear Miranda,

As far as I know, you don't become a lesbian or bisexual overnight. Only you know how you feel inside. It seems to me that this woman who seduced you is your exception to the rule. You say you were happily married but does a happily married woman allow herself to become seduced by a stranger? Is it possible you were happy overall but lacking excitement in the bedroom?

I think the more important question here might be what to do about your husband. Are you going to tell him or keep your affair a secret? It seems you have a lot to consider and I have offered you more questions than answers. C'est la vie.

"Une serrure ne s'ouvre qu'avec la bonne clé." — French Proverb

"A lock only opens with the right key."

Letter 58

I have been married 10 years and I feel stuck but I am terrified at the thought of starting over. Do I continue in this loveless marriage for the sake of the children or should I find the courage to move on?

Colleen
Leipsic, OH

Dear Colleen,

This is a dilemma that I have seen too many times in America. Women find themselves trapped in a bad marriage for the children or for financial reasons, or both. I do notice a difference between French and American women. A French woman can leave a bad marriage without a great deal of worrying about tomorrow because health care and day care are universal and the government is very involved in peoples' lives. French women seem to receive more encouragement to be independent if they choose to be.

Women in America do not always have that level of support. An American woman has to weigh the good and the bad, at the risk of being a martyr to protect her children.

I will not tell you what to do. A few lines of information are not enough to offer life-altering advice, but I will plead with you to never let fear get in the way of doing what you know is right.

"Mieux vaut être oiseau des bois que de cage."
— French Proverb

"It is better to be a bird in the wild rather than a caged bird."

I know what it's like to feel stuck in a marriage. That was how I felt only five years into my own. I never married with the intention of divorcing one day. Nobody does. Nothing feels more wonderful than to meet someone and fall in love.

Having parents who divorced when I was a child, I never wanted my children to have the same experience. My father was a champion of libertinage. He changed partners as often as he changed his shirt. Experiencing the tension between my parents was unbelievably stressful. Walking away from my marriage was not an option for me. I stayed for the children. Looking back, it was a bad decision. Although my marriage was not sexless, there was no reciprocity of love in our relationship. I felt a sense of relief when my wife made the first move toward divorce because I could not. Today, I know that my children are better off with two happy parents who live in separate homes than they would have been with two miserable parents under the same roof.

Letter 59

I am drawn to alpha males and domination, but sometimes I wonder if dating men with less intensity would make relationships easier. Would you agree?

DeShawn
Royal Oak, MI

Dear DeShawn,

No, I would not agree. Going against what you are attracted to is depriving yourself of what you truly enjoy.

Agreed, alpha males are more intense and relationships with them can be more challenging. However, you and I both know that there is nothing more exhilarating for a woman with your attraction to dominance than to be taken by a true alpha male who knows how to put you in your place the way no one else can. Why deny yourself of your deepest pleasure?

I have to make a very important disclaimer here because not every alpha male is a true man. Those two things can be mutually exclusive. A true man knows how to dominate his submissive partner with respect. If a dominant man is not making you happy, he is not the one for you. Don't give up on what you like. There are others to choose from.

"Il faut être soi-même pour pouvoir aimer."
— *French Proverb*

"You have to be yourself to be able to love."

I don't define myself in terms of alpha or beta. I never worry about being perceived in those terms and I will not change my true nature to impress another. I would describe myself as a strong man with a good soul. I have been on many dates with American women. A chivalrous spirit during courtship is part of the French culture. Unfortunately, some women misinterpret that spirit as weakness. I am often taken aback by how surprised some American women become at the smallest romantic or chivalrous gestures. I live life with the attitude of a lion. A lion doesn't turn around when dogs bark.

Letter 60

On a second date with a man, he took me to a restaurant and then to the movies. A few minutes into the movie, with no one else in the theater, he stood up in front of me, unzipped his pants, and told me to "suck it." I was pretty scared, but I said "no" and he drove me home. That kind of thing makes a woman nervous to date. He was nice up to that point. I never saw that behavior coming. After coming out of a 25-year marriage, is this what I have to look forward to? Is this the new dating norm?

Chloe
Baton Rouge, LA

Dear Chloe,

Merde! I am disturbed by your experience and even more so that you got into a car with this man. You are fortunate that your date didn't end much worse. Dating sites are infested with predators. Women go online to find love and find themselves lost in the woods in the middle of the night without survival gear.

My advice to you when dating online is to avoid free dating sites. Spend a few dollars on a better-rated site. This will not make you immune to scammers and liars but it should increase the pool of good men. And please, never get into a car with a date on your first time meeting. Arrange to meet in a public place. Don't invite a man into your home until every fiber of your being tells you it feels right. Trust your gut.

Don't give up. Don't let a few bad experiences keep you from putting yourself out there. I know a woman who runs background checks on all of her dates beforehand. It doesn't cost much to do that these days. The most surprising result she got back was from a man with a 24-year prison history. You may have to sift through the mud to find a few gems but the gems are out there.

My friend, Darcy, is a funny woman. Her dating stories are very entertaining at gatherings. She describes online dating like this:

"Online dating is 90 percent comedy and 10 percent luck. I have had the best tears-rolling-down-my-face laughs while reading dating profiles and swiping through profile pictures. It almost seems like some men are actively trying to repel women. A few of the things that will earn my immediate shutdown are profile pics without a shirt, with a headboard background, where I can see a toilet, or sporting a dead animal as a trophy, excessively bad grammar, the word 'conversate,' biographies that took zero effort or are blank, and consistent misuse of the words 'your,' 'you're,' 'there,' 'they're,' 'their,' 'to,' and 'too.'

"There are three types of men on dating sites. The first type are scammers. They are looking for vulnerable, lonely women with full wallets. The second type are players. They are the men looking to get laid. These men are 'SSS,' strictly seeking sex. The players are divided into two subcategories. Men in Category A are honest about not wanting a relationship. They will tell you they are not looking for anything serious. That is code for 'I just want to fuck.'

Category B are liars. They appear to want a relationship. They will say everything they think you want to hear so that they can land in bed with you. These men are planning to hit it and quit it. The third type are genuinely good men seeking good women. There are way fewer men of that third type. Finding them is similar to finding a needle in a haystack but not impossible. Expect to sift through ones, twos, two-As, two-Bs, and threes during the course of online dating.

"I once let a man stick me with the dinner bill on our first date. The check came and he suddenly had a glazed look in his eyes. His head dropped a little, as if he was communicating telepathically with his shoelaces. I sat there for a minute and looked at this fool in amazement. I could have made a scene and walked out, but I decided to take the high road and pull out my wallet. His eyes cleared up the minute the waitress took my credit card. He thanked me for dinner and we headed our separate ways. A couple of days later, he called me and said he had had a wonderful time and was looking forward to seeing me again. *Insert tears-rolling-down-my-face laugh here!* I told him we would not go out again. He then asked why. I told him I wasn't used to being treated that way. He played it off like I was making a big deal out of nothing. He said, 'So, let me get this right. You don't want to see me again because you paid for *a* dinner?' To which I replied, 'I didn't pay for *a* dinner. I paid for our *first* dinner. There's a difference. If that was the first impression you chose to make, I'm not interested in seeing the rest. Take care of yourself.' He called a few more times after that conversation but I never picked up. I'm not sure what he was trying to prove, but I do know people will treat you the way you let them. I know my worth and I am more than happy to remain single if it means not compromising on what I am willing to put up with from a partner."

"Si 'arbre savait ce que lui réserve la hache, il ne lui fournirait pas la manche." — *French Proverb*

"If the tree knew what the ax had in mind, it would not provide it with the handle."

Conclusion

Merci beaucoup to everyone who shared a piece of their personal life in the form of a letter. I am humbled by your demonstration of trust in me. Merci beaucoup to you, the reader. I hope you enjoyed reading this book as much as I enjoyed writing it. I learned a lot from each letter, and I did my very best to answer each one with sincerity and respect. Despite the cliché of the French lover, I am not an expert on women or relationships. I am not a spokesman. I am one Frenchman with a great curiosity about humanity and an observant eye for interpersonal relationships.

My hope is that something discussed in each letter has lifted at least one other person, if only to the extent of making them feel as though someone else understands them. Many French men and women may not agree with me; many may have had a different life experience, but different experiences are what make us unique and all of us are worthy of having our story heard.

Having lived in America with dual citizenship for many years, I have experienced the affection Americans have for France, Paris in particular. I feel the love when I am asked to translate a phrase into French, when people reminisce fondly about their trips to France, or when I am asked for recommendations for their next trips. I feel the love when people want to discuss my favorite pieces at the Louvre. I feel the love when I am asked about French cuisine, fashion, or politics. It warms my heart to see so many Americans with a fondness for my homeland. This love also compels me to add that, yes, there are differences between French and American culture, but fundamentally, we are all human beings with similar triumphs and struggles. We all want to live in peace, free to love and exist how we see fit.

This last wish is for my daughters as much as it is for all French and American women. I wish you the courage and drive to pursue your dreams relentlessly until they become a reality and to never lower your standards for how you deserve to be treated.

Merci,
Blaise

Acknowledgements

I would like to thank C. Raven Hernandez for assisting me in the creation of this book. Thank you Book Launchers for your kind support and expertise.

Made in United States
North Haven, CT
12 February 2022

16035456R00089